Bible reflections
for older people

BRF

The Bible Reading Fellowship
15 The Chambers, Vineyard
Abingdon OX14 3FE
brf.org.uk

The Bible Reading Fellowship (BRF) is a Registered Charity (233280)

ISBN 978 0 85746 515 3

Acknowledgements
Scripture quotations marked NIV are taken from The Holy Bible, New International Version (Anglicised edition), copyright © 1979, 1984, 2011 by Biblica. Used by permission of Hodder & Stoughton Publishers, an Hachette UK company. All rights reserved. 'NIV' is a registered trademark of Biblica. UK trademark number 1448790.

Scripture quotations marked NRSV are taken from the New Revised Standard Version of the Bible, Anglicised edition, copyright © 1989, 1995 by the Division of Christian Education of the National Council of the Churches of Christ in the United States of America. Used by permission. All rights reserved.

Scripture quotations marked RSV are taken from the Revised Standard Version of the Bible, copyright © 1946, 1952, and 1971 the Division of Christian Education of the National Council of the Churches of Christ in the United States of America. Used by permission. All rights reserved.

Scripture quotations marked NLT are taken from the Holy Bible, New Living Translation, copyright © 1996, 2004, 2007, 2013. Used by permission of Tyndale House Publishers, Inc., Carol Stream, Illinois 60188. All rights reserved.

Every effort has been made to trace and contact copyright owners for material used in this resource. We apologise for any inadvertent omissions or errors, and would ask those concerned to contact us so that full acknowledgement can be made in the future.

Printed by Gutenberg Press, Tarxien, Malta

Contents

About the writers

 Tony Horsfall has been a missionary and pastor, and now travels widely, speaking and leading retreats. He is a writer and mentor, and has a special concern for spiritual growth as people journey through life into maturity. He has written seven books for BRF, including *Rhythms of Grace*, *Working from a Place of Rest* and *Deep Calls to Deep*.

 Ann Lewin was a teacher of RE and English for 27 years. Now retired, she writes, leads Quiet Days and retreats and works with individuals and groups, helping people explore their spirituality. She has had experience of caring for people with dementia, first her mother and then one of her brothers, over a period of about 35 years.

 Emlyn Williams worked for many years for Scripture Union, latterly for SU International, and spent much of his time with Christians in Eastern Europe. He is a writer of many individual and group Bible materials, and is currently Discipleship Pastor working as part of the leadership team in a large Anglican church.

 Katherine Hedderly is Associate Vicar for Ministry at St Martin-in-the-Fields, London. She has developed the church's work on dementia, bringing together those with lived experience, healthcare practitioners and theologians. Before ordination she worked in broadcasting for 20 years, including as head of development for an independent production company.

From the Editor

Welcome! We hope you will find the Bible reflections in the following pages helpful and encouraging.

Whatever the challenges of the moment, writer **Tony Horsfall** encourages us to rest in God's love—knowing we're accepted and forgiven by him. **Ann Lewin**, poet and retreat leader, reminds us of God's enduring call to be fruitful even, or perhaps especially, in our later years. And for when things are particularly difficult, **Emlyn Williams** gently reminds us that God walks with us through the painful times of our lives. Finally, **Katherine Hedderly** reassures us that whether life is full or we feel alone, we are known and loved by God.

In the centre pages, **Debbie Thrower** of **BRF's The Gift of Years** ministry brings stories, ideas, encouragement and a wonderful poem by Grace Westerduin. We hope you will enjoy reading these and hearing from others who may be facing similar issues to your own.

As you read these Bible reflections and spend time with God, we pray that you will know his presence and also that sense of his love which, as our first series reminds us, holds us safe: 'The eternal God is your refuge, and underneath are the everlasting arms' (Deuteronomy 33:27, NIV).

God bless you,

Tricia Williams

From the September 2017 issue, *Bible Reflections for Older People* will be edited by **Eley McAinsh**.

Using these reflections

Perhaps you have always had a special daily time for reading the Bible and praying. But now, as you grow older, you are finding it more difficult to keep to a regular pattern or find it hard to concentrate. Or maybe you've never done this before. Whatever your situation, these Bible reflections aim to help you take a few moments to read God's word and pray, whenever you are able.

When to read them

You can read these Bible reflections in the morning or last thing at night, or any time during the day. Why not use them as a way of making 'an appointment to chat with God'?

There are 40 daily Bible reflections, grouped around four themes. Each one includes some verses from the Bible, a reflection to help you in your own thinking about God and a suggestion for prayer. The reflections aren't dated, so it doesn't matter if you're not able to read them every day. The Bible verses are printed, but if you'd like to read from your own Bible, that's fine too.

How to read them

- **Take time** to quieten yourself, becoming aware of God's presence, asking him to speak to you through the Bible and the reflection.

- **Read** the Bible verses and the reflection:
  - What do you especially like or find helpful in these verses?
  - What might God be saying to you through this reading?
  - Is there something to pray about or thank God for?

- **Pray**. Each reflection includes a prayer suggestion. You might like to pray for yourself or take the opportunity to think about and pray for others.

Resting in God's love

Tony Horsfall

I wonder if you have discovered the benefits of a good armchair? Perhaps one that is soft and comforting and, when positioned by a window, becomes your favourite place in the house? Or one that reclines at the touch of a button and, at the flick of a switch, sets you on your feet again? Such chairs are not cheap, but are a sound investment in later years!

The theme of these readings is 'resting in God's love'. As you read, find a comfortable place to sit and relax, and imagine yourself surrounded and supported by this great love. Begin with these words from Deuteronomy 33:27: 'The eternal God is your refuge, and underneath are the everlasting arms' (NIV).

Just as we can be enveloped in a cosy armchair, so we can be enfolded in the love of God.

At every stage of life, we need to be reminded that we are loved by God. Such awareness brings us comfort, makes us compassionate and gives us courage for each new day.

1 John 4:8, 16 (NIV)

The nature of God

Whoever does not love does not know God, because God is love... And so we know and rely on the love God has for us. God is love. Whoever lives in love lives in God, and God in them.

How would you introduce yourself? Sometimes it's not easy to know what to include—or to leave out. The apostle John introduced himself as 'the disciple whom Jesus loved'. It was the thing he was most sure about when it came to his identity (John 13:23; 19:26; 20:2; 21:7, 20).

John's certainty was not based upon any confidence he had in his being lovable, or feeling he had somehow earned or deserved such love. It came from his knowledge of the character and nature of God. This assurance he shares in his epistle. Twice he declares: 'God is love.' It is the best definition we have of God, and the foundation for our understanding of him.

We too can say that we are loved by God, not because of what we have done (or not done) but because of who God is. God is love and we are the objects of that love, like when the sun shines on us and, without effort on our part, we feel its warmth.

■ PRAYER

Father, help me to rest today in the assurance of your love for me. I don't need to earn your love and I can never forfeit it. Amen

John 3:16–17 (NIV)

Love that gives

For God so loved the world that he gave his one and only Son, that whoever believes in him shall not perish but have eternal life. For God did not send his Son into the world to condemn the world, but to save the world through him.

Love is at the heart of who God is—not just a characteristic, but the very essence of his being. It is the nature of love to want to give, to help those in need, even though that may be costly.

These verses from John, sometimes called 'the gospel in a nutshell', encapsulate the good news of the Christian message. God could not remain passive before human sinfulness and failure. His love compelled him to do something to save us, and found its expression in sending his Son, Jesus, to be the Saviour of the world.

Sharing that same love, the Son of God entered our world willingly, ready to lay down his life for us. God is reluctant that any should miss out on eternal life. The loving sacrifice of Father and Son has meant that now no one need perish. The only question is whether or not we will recognise that love at work on our behalf, and receive the gift it offers.

■ **PRAYER**

Lord, I am moved because you were moved—moved to see my plight, and moved to come to my rescue by sending your Son to save me. Cause me to love you in return. Amen

Psalm 103:8–12 (NIV)

Love that forgives and forgets

The Lord is compassionate and gracious, slow to anger, abounding in love. He will not always accuse, nor will he harbour his anger for ever; he does not treat us as our sins deserve or repay us according to our iniquities. For as high as the heavens are above the earth, so great is his love for those who fear him; as far as the east is from the west, so far has he removed our transgressions from us.

I don't have many regrets in life, but I do wish I had continued to play sport and develop whatever talent I had. For various reasons, I didn't, which in retrospect was a mistake.

I wonder if you have regrets? Regret is a common problem for many of us as we grow older. It's tempting to look back and ask ourselves, 'What if?' or, 'If only…' Yet this tendency to rake over the old ground of past decisions, mistakes and failures is unhelpful—and one of the surest ways into depression. We cannot change the past, only accept it and move on.

The psalmist reminds us of the forgiving grace of God. He can bring good out of past mistakes and forgive any failures or wrongdoing. If God is willing to forgive us, then we must learn to forgive ourselves as well. That may be the hardest part.

■ PRAYER

Lord, thank you for your forgiveness, and the grace that covers my mistakes. Amen

Romans 5:6–8 (NIV)

Love demonstrated

You see, at just the right time, when we were still powerless, Christ died for the ungodly. Very rarely will anyone die for a righteous person, though for a good person someone might possibly dare to die. But God demonstrates his own love for us in this: while we were still sinners, Christ died for us.

A friend is currently undergoing treatment for cancer. It is like passing through a long dark tunnel, coping with side effects and the uncertainty surrounding the diagnosis. At such times, it can be easy to lose sight of God's love. Indeed, we may begin to wonder if God loves us at all.

When feelings no longer support the fact of God's love, and circumstances seemingly contradict it, we can turn our eyes again to the cross. Calvary presents us with an objective demonstration of the love of God, with the historical reminder that God has loved us and will continue to do so. There is no reason to doubt that love when we remember how the Son of God gave himself to die for us, as it says in Galatians 2:20.

The choice remains to rest on the objective fact of God's love displayed through the cross, rather than be led by our subjective emotions or changing circumstances. This is not easy, but is made possible by the wonderful grace of God.

■ **PRAYER**

Lord, keep my eyes fixed on you through the changing scenes of life, trusting in your love even when I don't feel it. Amen

Romans 5:3–5 (NIV, 1984)

Love received

Not only so, but we also rejoice in our sufferings, because we know that suffering produces perseverance; perseverance, character; and character, hope. And hope does not disappoint us, because God has poured out his love into our hearts by the Holy Spirit, whom he has given us.

My wife and I were recently sent a surprise gift. It came by courier, but was delivered to the wrong address. Eventually, when we discovered it had gone to a neighbour's house, we retrieved it unopened, and belatedly enjoyed this very special gift—a box of expensive chocolates!

God wants us to know his love as an objective fact, but he also wants us to feel it in our hearts. Feelings are not everything, but they matter, and the Holy Spirit has been given the task of making God's love real to us. This he does by pouring God's love into our hearts so that we *know* we are loved.

This work of the Spirit may be experienced gradually as a growing realisation over time (like a steady drizzle), or as a sudden, personal awareness of God's love (like being drenched in a thunderstorm). Either way, God wants us to enjoy the 'blessed assurance' that Fanny Crosby (1820–1915) spoke about in her great hymn of the same name. It is a generous gift from our Father, to be received thankfully.

■ **PRAYER**

Lord, grant that I may know your love in both my head and my heart, and share it with others. Amen

Psalm 57:9–10 (NIV)

Great is thy faithfulness

I will praise you, Lord, among the nations; I will sing of you among the peoples. For great is your love, reaching to the heavens; your faithfulness reaches to the skies.

I recently returned to the city in Malaysia where I began my ministry as a missionary pastor some 40 years ago. It was encouraging to see that many of those who were young people in that fledgling congregation are still strong and active in their faith. The church too has grown and matured. Together, we thanked God for his faithfulness over many years.

The faithfulness of God is an expression of his unchanging love, and was the basis of the covenant he made with his people in the Old Testament. In Hebrew there is a special word for this, *hesed*, usually translated as 'steadfast love'. We can count on God because he is committed to us in love. Even when we are faithless, he remains faithful.

Looking back over your life, I hope that you too can see this same faithfulness at work. No wonder 'Great is thy faithfulness' (Thomas Chisholm, 1866–1960) is such a popular hymn. It helps us to express our gratitude for God's unfailing love and to join the psalmist in declaring to a younger generation that God can indeed be trusted.

■ **PRAYER**

Lord, you are faithful; you have been faithful; and you will be faithful. Help me to remember this when times are hard and the way is uncertain. Amen

Romans 8:38–39 (NIV)

The love that holds us secure

For I am convinced that neither death nor life, neither angels nor demons, neither the present nor the future, nor any powers, neither height nor depth, nor anything else in all creation, will be able to separate us from the love of God that is in Christ Jesus our Lord.

I am in the process of scaling down my library. It's not easy because books are like friends to me. But I realise as I get older that I have to deal with the 'stuff' in my life so it will not become a burden for others. The attic, however, must wait!

Ageing involves a series of losses as we let go of things that have been part of our lives. This includes relationships too, as people we have known and loved pass away. Grief is an inevitable emotion in later years and it can make us feel depressed or insecure about the future.

The apostle Paul's precious words remind us that we will never be separated from the love of God. No matter what happens, the grip of grace on our lives will hold firm and strong. We may become physically or mentally frail, but his love surrounds us like a shield and his presence is our strength. Here is a truth to rest upon whenever you feel afraid or alone: nothing, absolutely nothing, can separate you from God's amazing love.

■ **PRAYER**

Lord, in my weakest moments you are my strength. Amen

Ephesians 3:17–19 (NIV, 1984)

A prayer for love

And I pray that you, being rooted and established in love, may have power, together with all the saints, to grasp how wide and long and high and deep is the love of Christ, and to know this love that surpasses knowledge—that you may be filled to the measure of all the fullness of God.

We may not always know how to help our friends and loved ones when they are in need, but we can always pray for them. Here is a prayer which speaks to everyone's deepest need: to understand and experience the immensity of God's love.

Words fail the apostle Paul as he tries to describe the vastness of God's love. Mathematically, it's impossible for an object to have four dimensions at the same time (length, width, height, depth)! But God's love is immeasurable.

Then he adds another impossibility—that we might be filled with God's fullness. No human being can contain God's fullness, at least not without overflowing! Perhaps that's the point—that we become so full of love, it spills over to other people.

Stability in life comes as we allow ourselves to be rooted (like a tree) in the soil of God's love, and established (like a building) on this firm foundation. That means taking time regularly to sit quietly and receive God's great love into our lives.

■ **PRAYER**

Lord, make God's love real in my life and in the lives of those for whom I pray. Amen

Ephesians 5:1–2 (NIV, 1984)

Living a life of love

Be imitators of God, therefore, as dearly loved children and live a life of love, just as Christ loved us and gave himself up for us as a fragrant offering and sacrifice to God.

Our church has just celebrated its 25th birthday. We began with a dozen people, mostly in their 40s and 50s. Now we are in our 60s and 70s! While the church has grown slowly over the years, this same group of pioneers are still actively involved.

Many smaller churches depend, like us, on an active band of older people. Our pastor reminds us to pace ourselves: 'Do what you can, when you can,' he says. It's great to see the 'life of love' being lived out in faithful service week by week. The love of God so freely received motivates us to love and care for others.

Active service is not always possible, however. We may become housebound and unable to take part in church life as once we did. Whatever our circumstances, we can still live a life of love. It can be expressed in our thoughtfulness, kind words, generous giving, prayerful interest, encouraging phone calls and even in a smile and cheery disposition. The love of God is not bound in any way and, if we allow it, his love will find its own unique expression in our lives.

■ **PRAYER**

Lord, help me, as I am able, to live a life of love. Amen

Jude 20–21 (NIV, 1984)

The only place to be

But you, dear friends, build yourselves up in your most holy faith and pray in the Holy Spirit. Keep yourselves in God's love as you wait for the mercy of our Lord Jesus Christ to bring you to eternal life.

In the course of my ministry I have travelled a great deal, visited numerous fascinating countries and met many wonderful people. I enjoy travelling, but I am always ready to come home. As the saying goes, 'Home is where the heart is.'

In spiritual terms, home is where we find our resting place in God. It is the place within us where we know ourselves to be loved by God, unreservedly and without condition. It is here we need to return again and again, whenever we feel that we have wandered.

Jesus spoke about the importance of abiding in him: 'As the Father has loved me, so I have loved you; abide in my love' (John 15:9, NRSV). To abide is to make one's abode. As believers we are to make our home, our dwelling place, in the love of God (Psalm 90:1; 91:1).

Jude reminds us here of the part we play in strengthening our faith. We are to stay where God has placed us, in the centre of his love. This is our resting place and our true home.

◼ **PRAYER**

Lord, help me to cultivate this place of intimacy with you. Keep me anchored in your love, I pray. Amen

Fruitfulness

Ann Lewin

Our older years are potentially rich. It's true that they are not without challenges, as the media keep telling us. As a society we are going to have to think hard about how best we can support people into their later years. But the wisdom which comes with maturity can keep us hopeful.

I have been struck in recent years by the verse near the end of Psalm 92, 'They will still bear fruit in old age' (v. 14, NIV), words which have given me hope as awareness of mortality has increased. This idea of fruitfulness, as expressed in scripture, can help us to grow through the experience of ageing.

This series begins with a recognition that being chosen by Jesus is for a purpose: bearing fruit. Fruitfulness takes many forms, but if we are to have the kind of senior moment that Simeon and Anna had when the baby Jesus was presented at the Temple (Luke 2:22–40), we need to pay attention to God, and root ourselves in his love. We need to abide in the life of Christ who gives us growth, recognising that our declining years are part of the natural rhythm of life in which death plays a part in ensuring new growth.

Fruitfulness is multifaceted, and undergirding all aspects of our relationship with God is thankfulness, which keeps our faces turned to the light of God's love, and enables us to grow.

John 15:12, 14, 16 (NRSV)

Being chosen

Love one another as I have loved you… You are my friends if you do what I command you… You did not choose me but I chose you. And I appointed you to go and bear fruit, fruit that will last.

Do you remember being in the playground when teams were being picked? There was always the fear of being left until last! Perhaps later, there have been more serious experiences: not getting a job we wanted, or being rejected by someone we loved. Over and against all these, Jesus says, 'I chose you.'

We often get our discipleship the wrong way round, thinking that we chose to follow Jesus. But our following is always in response to his call. We are called into a new relationship: to be God's friends. The 'you' in this passage is plural. We are not chosen to be 'special friends', in a relationship which excludes everyone else. We are not going to be spoilt—we are entrusted with a responsibility: to bear fruit.

Bearing fruit in the natural world comes at the end of a process of growth. Yet there are many points in our lives when fruitfulness is displayed. We are being prepared through all of our lives to bear the fruit of love: 'Love one another as I have loved you,' Jesus said. Such costly love will transform our relationships and, ultimately, the world around us.

■ **PRAYER**

Lord, help us to believe that you love us, and help us to love others because you love them too. Amen

Psalm 92:12, 14 (NIV)

Being fruitful

The righteous will flourish… They will still bear fruit in old age, they will stay fresh and green.

For many people, a significant form of fruitfulness comes through establishing and caring for a family. There is, of course, great satisfaction in watching children grow up and produce the next generation. But not everyone has that blessing to enjoy, and it can be hard to rejoice with those who have grand- and great-grandchildren, as they show their photos and share stories.

Having children is just one way to create life and 'bear fruit'. There are many kinds of creativity which enable people to flourish themselves, and to draw out creativity in others. And these verses reassure us that we can go on 'being fruitful' even in 'old age'.

Our creative gifts are never ours for our own satisfaction, but are all ways in which love can be expressed, and our community encouraged. It may be that we can offer hospitality or time, a listening ear or a friendly smile. Or we can share our skills and encourage others to develop theirs—a sharing of gifts which can span the generations. All of these, whether they seem trivial or play a big part in our lives, can bring us great joy as we work with God to bring light and life to those around us.

■ PRAYER

Creator God, fill us with your Spirit, so that we are enabled to use our gifts to your glory and for the good of all around us. Amen

Ephesians 3:17–19 (RSV)

Roots and fruits

... that you, being rooted and grounded in love, may... know the love of Christ which surpasses knowledge, that you may be filled with all the fullness of God.

You may have moved house recently—or be about to do so. It's not always a matter of choice, and it can feel like being uprooted. Some of us don't transplant easily: it takes time for us to put down roots, to find out how we belong in our new context and how we can contribute to its life.

Paul wrote to the Christians in Ephesus about a kind of rootedness that doesn't depend on outward circumstances, but which can transform our attitude to them. He prayed that they would be rooted in the love of Christ.

Our fruitfulness depends on our having a good root system, and it is prayer that carries the nourishment God gives us through his love to the whole of our being. Prayer is the lifeblood of our relationship with God, taking us to the source of our life, and giving us the energy to produce fruit appropriate to our stage of life.

Wherever we are on our life's journey, we need to nurture our relationship with God—through time in God's company, putting our roots down into his love. Whatever else may change, God will never let us go.

■ PRAYER

We pray for all who have been uprooted from their settled way of life, that they will be sustained by God's love and find opportunities to be fruitful again. Amen

John 15:1–2 (RSV)

Being pruned

I am the true vine, and my Father is the vinedresser. Every branch of mine that bears no fruit, he takes away, and every branch that does bear fruit he prunes, that it may bear more fruit.

I used to think it strange that my father pinched out the tops of tomato plants. He said it encouraged the plants to concentrate on producing fruit. It seemed such a waste. Of course, he was right. Left to themselves, plants sometimes squander their energy, keeping alive parts of themselves which are not going to be fruitful.

Jesus describes our relationship with him as being like the relationship of branches to a vine. We are dependent on him, the main stem, for our life, and are intended to bear fruit. Any branch that does not bear fruit is cut out, and the healthy branches are trimmed so that they focus on fruiting.

In life this process goes on all the time, and it can be painful as we lose what has been precious to us. It can be hard as we grow older to bid farewell to things we once held dear, for example, being active members of a church. But being less active doesn't mean not being fruitful. The life Jesus gives us when we stay close to him can result in fruitfulness as we allow the Spirit to grow us further.

■ **PRAYER**

'For all that has been, thanks. To all that shall be, yes.' Amen

* Dag Hammarskjöld (1905–1961)

Galatians 5:22–23 (NIV)

The fruit we hope to bear

But the fruit of the Spirit is love, joy, peace, forbearance, kindness, goodness, faithfulness, gentleness and self-control.

Letting God's Spirit bring us to fruitfulness opens up all kinds of possibilities. The apostle Paul had been writing to the Galatian Christians about the things which destroy community and make it hard for people to flourish. Then he listed the attributes quoted above. All are gifts from God which not only enhance our own well-being, but help build relationships and enable others to grow too.

The more we allow these qualities to be developed in us, the more we grow. None of them is easy to demonstrate—but that is a reminder that we are not the ones who initiate their growth; we are dependent on God.

Some of these qualities may already be quite well developed in us. Others need encouragement. It might be a profitable exercise to ask the Spirit to show us where we need to grow, and to give us the grace to attempt one expression of that quality each day. For example: a kind word to someone who annoys us, not retaliating when someone hurts us. It will become clear to us where we need to grow as we become more aware of the effect we have on people around us. And faithfulness will keep us gently focused on allowing God's Spirit to fill us with his love.

■ PRAYER

Open us up, Lord, to the prompting of your Spirit, and give us grace to enable others to flourish. Amen

Luke 2:25, 36–37 (RSV)

A senior moment

There was a man in Jerusalem, whose name was Simeon, and this man was righteous and devout, looking for the consolation of Israel, and the Holy Spirit was upon him… And there was a prophetess, Anna… she was of a great age, having lived with her husband [for] seven years… and as a widow till she was eighty-four.

The story of Simeon and Anna is a great encouragement as we grow older—it's one of the few occasions in the Bible when older people get the best lines!

Simeon and Anna saw embodied in the six-week-old baby brought to the Temple by Mary and Joseph the culmination of all their hopes and longings. This was the fulfilment of God's promise made to his people long before—and their response was to speak of their belief that God was at work (Luke 2:29–32).

Their constant attention to God in prayer and worship in the Temple; their expectation that God would act in a not very promising political and social context; their alertness to the possibility that God might work in an unexpected way—all had prepared them for this moment of recognition—a senior moment to die for.

As the psalmist wrote: 'planted in the house of the Lord, they flourish… They still bring forth fruit in old age' (Psalm 92:13–14, RSV).

■ **PRAYER**

Lord, keep us alert to the possibility that you will be found in unlikely places and people; help us to keep faith alive when those around us despair. Amen

2 Corinthians 4:16 (NRSV)

Still growing

So we do not lose heart. Even though our outer nature is wasting away, our inner nature is being renewed day by day.

'Who'd have thought that I'd go funny in the head like this?' my mother said in one of her more lucid moments, as dementia increased its hold on her.

People used to talk about the stage of life when physical and mental capacities dwindle as 'second childhood'. But childhood is a time for developing new skills, widening our horizons. Old age can be a cruel reversal of that, as one by one abilities and independence are lost.

Loss of memory, dementia and bewilderment can be hard to bear, certainly hard to watch—and dementia is no respecter of persons. But thinking only in terms of loss is not helpful. Perhaps, as Revd Sam Wells suggested on BBC Radio 4's *Thought for the Day* programme,[*] underneath the apparent confusion there is growth. Eternal life is a gift given in this life which comes to fruition in the fullness of God's presence the other side of death. Perhaps this stage is not so much second childhood as a positive 'third age'.

Holding on to this hope for those for whom we care is a positive contribution to what might otherwise be a wilderness experience.

■ **PRAYER**

Lord, help us to see the person behind the present confusion—and if our own faculties are beginning to be less sharp, help us to trust in your unfailing love and care. Amen

[*] Broadcast 22 September 2015

Ecclesiastes 3:1 (NRSV)

Have we got time?

For everything there is a season, and a time for every matter under heaven.

I remember painting the church railings, a tedious job if ever there was one! After what seemed like an hour, I discovered I'd only been at it for ten minutes. At other times, caught up in something, I've been amazed at where time has gone. Time is slippery: we have it, or we don't; we keep it, lose it, make it; give it, take it; don't know where it has gone; it flies, it drags—all in the framework of 24 hours. How is time for you now? Is it hanging heavy? Do we need to find a way of using it constructively?

The apostle Paul suggested that we pray always (1 Thessalonians 5:17). That may sound like a tall order—there are other things we have to do in the day too. But prayer is not confined to saying words; it's also about growing in a relationship. Julian of Norwich, a wise woman of the twelfth century, said that God delights in our prayer and wants it. Rowan Williams said it's like sunbathing, relaxing into the warmth and light of God's love. It's how God nourishes us in our relationship with him.

When time hangs heavy, it's an opportunity to remember that we are chosen and precious. Let that truth sink in, and be thankful.

■ PRAYER

Lord, when life seems to have no purpose, nourish us with your life and love, and help us to grow. Amen

Ecclesiastes 3:1–2 (NRSV)

A time to die?

For everything there is a season… a time to be born, and a time to die; a time to plant, and a time to pluck up what is planted.

As we grow older, we become more aware of our mortality, sometimes through experiencing a life-threatening illness, or simply because the number on the birthday cards gets larger! How do we respond to the realisation that we are going to die? Practically, we can make sure that our affairs are in order. But what about the inner preparation we can make?

The natural world lives by the rhythms of the life cycle: plants and trees demonstrate that death precedes new growth. For human beings things are more complex; life beyond death is a mystery. But the Christian faith holds this as one of its central beliefs: eternal life, which begins in our relationship with God now, carries us through death to what lies beyond.

We have only a few clues as to what life after death might be like. But Jesus said that he was going through death to prepare a place for us to be in God's presence for eternity (John 14:1–2). We can view death as a terminus, a heart-stopping jolt at the end of the line, or as a junction where faith catches the connection to be with God for ever.

■ **PRAYER**

Lord, help us to remember that your love will always hold us, and we need not be afraid. Amen

Philippians 4:4, 6–7 (NRSV)

In everything give thanks

Rejoice in the Lord always; again I will say, Rejoice… Do not worry about anything, but in everything by prayer and supplication with thanksgiving let your requests be made known to God. And the peace of God, which surpasses all understanding, will guard your hearts and your minds in Christ Jesus.

'Count your blessings, name them one by one,' says the old hymn by Johnson Oatman Jr (1897). But life can throw some hard things at us, and sometimes we feel overwhelmed. Practising thanksgiving can help us get things back in perspective. The apostle Paul's words make a helpful distinction: he doesn't tell us to give thanks *for* everything, but *in* everything.

There are some experiences, like illness or losing loved ones, which might make talk of being thankful seem out of the question. We may feel completely abandoned. But even in the darkest times when we feel alone, God walks with us and carries us: 'underneath are the everlasting arms' (Deuteronomy 33:27, NIV). We may not realise that until well after the event which caused us pain, but it's true.

Thanksgiving is not always something we feel. It is an act of will, an attitude we have to practise, like all God's gifts. But to be thankful reminds us that whatever life throws at us, God is faithful. His love will always hold us, and we need not be afraid.

■ PRAYER

'Thou that hast giv'n so much to me, give one thing more, a gratefull heart.'* Amen

* George Herbert (1593–1633), 'Gratefulnesse', 1633

The Gift of Years

 Debbie Thrower is Team Leader of BRF's
The Gift of Years ministry and an Anna Chaplain
to Older People working in care homes. Visit
thegiftofyears.org.uk to find out more.

Debbie writes...

Hello, and welcome to our latest set of reflections! As part of The Gift of Years—'resourcing the spiritual journey of older people'—I know how important it is to hear from fellow 'pilgrims' along the way. Visiting people, listening to their stories, is part of what I used to do as a broadcaster and now do as an Anna Chaplain. Our work is growing across the country, with Anna Chaplains in Hampshire, Lancashire, Kent and an increasing number of other places.

After the visitors have left, reading reflections like these and taking the opportunity to think more deeply may bring benefits you hadn't expected. One reader told me how she dips into her copy last thing at night. She told me that the words enable her to sleep more soundly, knowing 'I'm not alone in my thoughts'.

I hope our authors' words, and those in these centre pages, will give you a sense, too, that you journey along with companions who share many of the same concerns and, perhaps, difficult choices. I pray that they bring you insights, refreshment and, yes, companionship, especially for the steeper parts of life's journey.

With best wishes, *Debbie*

Meet writer Tony Horsfall...

 Tony Horsfall has been a missionary and pastor and now travels widely, speaking and leading retreats. He has a special concern for spiritual growth as people journey through life into maturity. Tony has written several books for BRF, including *Rhythms of Grace*, *Working from a Place of Rest* and *Deep Calls to Deep*, and wrote the series 'Resting in God's love' in these Bible reflections.

We asked Tony to tell us about his journey of faith and his work.

Tony, how did you come to faith?
I was converted as a teenager in a little Methodist chapel in the small Yorkshire pit village where I grew up. Two young evangelists were visiting from Cliff College, and I think it was the first time I had heard the gospel clearly explained.

What brought you into your ministry as a writer?
At school I dreamt of being a sports journalist, but it never happened! Instead, I became a missionary, serving on the island of Borneo, and then pastored a local church in Yorkshire. I began exploring contemplative spirituality and was encouraged to share what I discovered in writing. The result was my first book, *Rhythms of Grace*. After that I couldn't stop writing!

What do you hope your books will achieve?
My great theme is the inner life. In all that I write I am trying to help people to develop their relationship with God, and to stay centred on him.

What have you learned about God's love as you've written the series 'Resting in God's love' for these Bible reflections?

I have been reminded how vast it is, and how strongly God wants to share that love with us, in whatever season of life we find ourselves. God's love for us does not diminish because we are older and less active than we used to be. It remains constant and unchanging.

In difficult times, how has God's love helped you?

Moving into the phase of 'semi-retirement', after a very active ministry with lots of travel and speaking engagements, has meant that I have needed to find my identity once again in who I am (God's deeply loved child), rather than in what I do. My wife, Evelyn, is currently undergoing cancer treatment for a second time. We have both been encouraged to know that nothing (even cancer) can separate us from the love of God.

What about those who are no longer able to be physically active?

When we are no longer as fit and able as we used to be, we have to allow God to love us as we are, and to remind ourselves that his love is in no way conditional upon what we do. This is when we most need to *rest* in God's love, and to learn contentment in our limitations. I take great comfort from the words of Psalm 103:13–14: 'As a father has compassion on his children, so the Lord has compassion on those who fear him; for he knows how we are formed, he remembers that we are dust' (NIV).

Bleak Day

When your day
is a cube of despair—
lead casket closing in
your soul to straitened time
and space—and where
you feel contracted fatally
to nothingness—don't air
(Pandora-lavish) that barbed swarm,
grievances non-retractable,
to sting, to curse the world!

Kneel down, shoot sheer a prayer
(past doubt's low ceiling,
through the fine hatch of possibility)
that He will come,
He, whom death's dungeon walls
And barred doors can't deter.

See! With His key
of golden-wrought surprise
He's instant there!
Your bleak day's now
A stage set for His company,
and His grace
to act on. Hear him swear
'Lo… I am with you always
all your days!'

Grace Westerduin, from *Vaulting the Treadmill*
(Arthur H. Stockwell, 2014; used with kind permission)

Grace Westerduin

Debbie Thrower reflects, and talks to poet **Grace Westerduin**.

We all have bleak days... Sometimes we find it hard to pick ourselves up and try to be more optimistic. This poem captures how a faith perspective can change our response to a given situation. Instead of reacting badly to unwelcome news or mundane irritations, we can shoot a brief prayer to God to show us a different way. **Grace Westerduin** talked to me about her poem:

'The poem is me talking to myself. I wrote it years ago when I was in a place where I had no congenial people to share with. I think it could have surfaced on any day when all the colours of life suddenly drained away, or during a hospital stay, or following bereavement. Clearly I didn't want the state of mind to continue, or spread—hence I mention Pandora's malign box.

'Then I must have recalled *Pilgrim's Progress* where Christian, imprisoned by Giant Despair, discovers the Key (Promise) which gets him out of Doubting Castle. For me the escape was to be similar—through sending up an arrow prayer. After all, even death could not hold Jesus. He could even turn up in closed rooms.

'Now, I was already feeling much better. Accepting and welcoming the divine presence changes everything. I began to feel set free by his grace to become part of a drama much bigger than my self-contained cell-life.'

For those bleak days, this poem helps us see how we might use each moment—here and *now*—and encounter the unexpected.

Thank God for Charlie!

 Di Wright is grandmother to four grandchildren ranging in age from their mid-20s to three years old. The youngest, Charlie, has Down's syndrome. His mum and dad, Vanessa and Jonny, live near Gloucester. **Debbie Thrower** asked Di, at her home in Alton, Hampshire, to tell her about her role as a grandmother, particularly in the light of Charlie's special needs.

'A bit of a shock'

When I first became a grandmother it was a bit of a shock because I thought I was far too young! But I was very excited and pleased. I love them all—all four—the same.

'You have this joy, and then this fear'

During Vanessa's pregnancy with Charlie, I worried more than I had with the others. I didn't feel good, somehow. When Jonny first rang us, he told us that things hadn't gone to plan... and then... you're frightened. You have this joy, and then this fear.

'Prayer moves you to a different place'

Our minister came round—on his day off actually—and said prayers with us, and that sort of settled me down. Prayer moves you to a different place; it doesn't make it right, but it brings you to a place where you can cope... Our prayers in the end were that whatever is the best thing for Charlie is what we wanted... not the best thing for us. Our church were so supportive. Belonging to a Christian community is, well... I don't know how people survive without it. We got great support from everyone in our church.

'Charlie has progressed so well'

He has hearing aids because of his deafness. He is learning Makaton* because he doesn't speak words as such, but he signs in Makaton. Children with Down's syndrome have weak muscles and their muscle structure really has to be built up. He goes to a special school and does swimming there.

'My faith has always been there'

When I was a child my mum said prayers with me and my brother every night. Going to church has never been a problem… I've never had a blinding revelation, but my faith has always been there in the background.

'God suffers when we suffer'

I've come to believe that God suffers when we suffer. I don't think he ever inflicts pain. A sense of humour has also helped!… He sends you people. That's how I think of God: he is with us in the form of people he sends to us. I can name times when people are alongside you, while you need it, and it's such a comfort.

'There's great joy… thank you to God'

When I see Charlie it's just a joy. There's great joy, and I say thank you to God, for bringing him this far, and for giving him the right parents. To them he is just their boy, and to us he is just our grandson, Charlie—and we love him. He makes us laugh and he makes us cry… And he has brought so much love to so many people. It is just joy, joy, joy, really!

* Makaton is a language programme using signs and symbols to help people to communicate. More information at: www.makaton.org

Postcards from Heaven

Talking to people in later life, it becomes apparent that growing older comes as a surprise to each of us. We never feel ourselves to be old on the inside! Whatever season of life you are in, here's a book to enjoy.

Postcards from Heaven (BRF, 2016) is created by writer and artist Ellie Hart to help us hear from God, especially when we're going through seasons of change and uncertainty. Full of beautiful pictures and refreshing words and ideas, this little book reminds us of the excitement and adventure of holding fast to the hope that lies ahead of us—the Christian hope of heaven.

Ellie describes how, when she is beside the sea, standing on the beach, she scoops up as much water as she can hold in her hands, and thinks:

> 'This is how much of God's presence, power and peace I have experienced so far.' Then I look out at the sea. The difference between the water I can hold in my hands and the contents of the Mediterranean Sea (and then the Atlantic Ocean) is beyond my ability to comprehend. That's how much more there is to explore of God, that's how much more he has for you. You just need to ask. (p. 71)

A spiritual compass

As you enjoy the summer months, Ellie's writing might act as a kind of spiritual compass as you navigate the (sometimes) choppy waters of growing older. These postcards dare us to see ourselves as travellers, pilgrims, voyagers bound for mysteries beyond…

Living through hard times

Emlyn Williams

Dad grew up during the depression years of the 1920s. Grandad was unemployed for much of the time and depended on his dole money. One day Grandma accidentally dropped a ten shilling note on the fire. It was all they had for the week.

She sent Dad, with her last few coins, to get some chips from the fish and chip shop. Takeaway food was cheap in those days! And, I suspect, she also prayed. Soon he came back, but not just with a few chips—he had fish and chips for the whole family. The shop owner didn't know the situation but decided to be generous!

I've noticed that people who lived through those years prioritised food and heat—my grandparents' house always seemed warm and there was always plenty to eat. Their hard times had taught them some important lessons about priorities. In Dad's case, he learned important lessons about trusting God.

All of us go through hard times, but they can change us for the better. In this series we'll hear from people who learned tough lessons, and hopefully we'll gain some wisdom and encouragement. Most important, we'll be reminded that even Jesus wasn't immune from suffering—he understands our pain.

2 Corinthians 1:3–4 (NIV)

Painful but not pointless

Praise be to the God and Father of our Lord Jesus Christ, the Father of compassion and the God of all comfort, who comforts us in all our troubles, so that we can comfort those in any trouble with the comfort we ourselves receive from God.

A friend recently lost his wife after many happy years of marriage. Even though she had been ill for some time, inevitably her death was a shock. Initially the support of friends and family and the busyness of the funeral buoyed Peter's spirits. But now he is alone and facing the reality of living without her.

Over the years he has helped many people in similar situations. Now it's his turn. Hard though things are, he realises that he is receiving the comfort from God of which he has often spoken to others (vv. 3–4a). But while previously it had been to some extent theoretical, now it's for real. He can speak about God's comfort from his own experience.

There is an old book called *Don't Waste Your Sorrows*. Here Paul is talking about a similar idea. What can seem like pointless, painful experiences can begin to take on meaning when we share God's comfort with others (v. 4b). Is there someone you can comfort today?

■ PRAYER

Thank you, Father, for the times when you have brought me comfort. Please lead me today to someone in need of that same comfort. Amen

Isaiah 43:1–2 (NIV)

I will be with you

*'Do not fear, for I have redeemed you; I have summoned you by name;
you are mine. When you pass through the waters, I will be with you;
and when you pass through the rivers, they will not sweep over you.
When you walk through the fire, you will not be burned; the flames
will not set you ablaze.'*

Difficult times can be lonely. Other people's experiences are not
exactly like ours, and it can feel that we have to carry our own pain.
That's why I try very hard not to say to people, 'I know how you feel,'
because I *don't* know how they feel! But we can aim to do what God
promises here (v. 2): we can try to walk with them through the storm.

If God promises to be with us in these major crises (floods, rivers,
fire), surely he will be with us in the smaller things too. Like a child
walking ahead of a parent, we don't always see or feel that God is
with us. But rest assured, he is. And there's one more important
reason why we can trust him: we belong to him (v. 1). We have been
bought at a price (1 Corinthians 6:20). Surely he is not going to let go
of someone (you!) whom he has bought at such great cost.

■ PRAYER
*Think of someone you know (it could be you) who is facing a very hard
time. Pray that today they will know afresh that the Lord is with them.*

John 9:1–3 (NIV)

Whose fault?

As he went along, he saw a man blind from birth. His disciples asked him, 'Rabbi, who sinned, this man or his parents, that he was born blind?' 'Neither this man nor his parents sinned,' said Jesus, 'but this happened so that the works of God might be displayed in him.'

Suffering usually makes us ask 'Why?' And we live in a time when, if something goes wrong, the usual response—of the media at least—is to put the blame on someone. But sometimes there isn't a simple answer. It's just how things are.

In this case, the disciples thought the answer was straightforward: the man was blind because he or his parents had sinned. (How they thought he had sinned before he was born I'm not sure!) But Jesus came at it from a different angle. This wasn't about *blame*; it was about *purpose*. Something good would come out of his blindness. It wasn't pointless. Through it, people would see just what God can do.

When we're suffering ourselves, comments from friends such as, 'There must be a purpose in it,' can seem simplistic and downright unhelpful. And yet... a friend of mine, facing serious illness, offered himself for a drug trial, not for his own benefit but because he wanted his own pain to bring good to others.

■ PRAYER

Heavenly Father, in my darkest hours, when I can't see why I am suffering, may others be strengthened through seeing you at work in me. Amen

Matthew 26:39, 42, 44 (NIV)

An honest prayer

Going a little farther, he fell with his face to the ground and prayed, 'My Father, if it is possible, may this cup be taken from me. Yet not as I will, but as you will'… He went away a second time and prayed, 'My Father, if it is not possible for this cup to be taken away unless I drink it, may your will be done'… So he left them and went away once more and prayed the third time, saying the same thing.

Suffering opens us to particular temptations and one is false guilt: 'I should be coping better'; 'I'm failing God—I should be strong.' As if our pain isn't enough, it's doubled by this sense that *we* should be doing better.

So it's good to remember that Jesus went through the pain of suffering too and would have avoided it if he possibly could. In Gethsemane, just before his death and while his weary disciples couldn't stay awake, he prayed honestly to his Father. He was 'sorrowful and troubled' (v. 37), 'overwhelmed with sorrow' (v. 38). He longed to be spared the suffering ahead and straightforwardly asked his Father to take the 'cup' of his suffering away.

God hears your honest prayer. Tell him how you feel. Ask him to act. Be open to whatever he sends. Pray as Jesus did.

■ PRAYER

Father, if it is possible… Father, if it is not possible… Father, whatever it is, may your will be done. Amen

1 Peter 4:12–13 (NIV)

Suffering with Christ

Dear friends, do not be surprised at the fiery ordeal that has come on you to test you, as though something strange were happening to you. But rejoice inasmuch as you participate in the sufferings of Christ, so that you may be overjoyed when his glory is revealed.

I visited Ukraine soon after the break-up of the Soviet Union. One Christian I met had trained as both a doctor and a pharmacist. Both times, he passed the exams but was not allowed to qualify because he was a Christian. On one May Day holiday, he took his church youth group into the forest for a meeting. The police found out and he was arrested. During his long prison sentence, he was slowly poisoned and lost the ability to walk.

Few of us will have suffered like that. But have you been mocked for your faith, or sometimes felt excluded by family and friends? Have you been humiliated for standing up for what was right? Peter says that when those things happen we shouldn't be surprised (v. 12). It goes with the territory. But it also comes with huge honour too. Like my Ukrainian friend, and countless others, we are 'partners with Christ in his suffering' (v. 13, NLT) and there is joy ahead!

■ PRAYER

Thank you, Lord, for the privilege of suffering with you. Please give your grace and peace to all your children who suffer today. Strengthen them with the hope of seeing your glory. Amen

Revelation 21:4 (NIV)

No more tears

'He will wipe every tear from their eyes. There will be no more death'
or mourning or crying or pain, for the old order of things has passed
away.

Sometimes pain and suffering are relatively temporary. They pass
and the memory fades, at least until the next time... Sadly, however,
some people's suffering seems interminable. I knew a couple whose
daughter experienced serious mental illness and was, consequently,
dependent on them until they died in their late 80s. There was no
release in this life.

This verse from Revelation, often read at funerals, is a glimpse into
the future that can sustain us in the harsh reality of the present.
While most of us, thankfully, experience lots of joy in our lives, there
is no certainty. In reality, pain and difficulty are never far off. They
can come at any time. No wonder people have spoken of life as the
'vale of tears'. But it is not the end. Here, the vision of John is about
much more than happier days when things have improved, like a
change in the weather.

What is ahead is nothing less than a new world where 'the old order
of things has passed away' (v. 4). Not only will our tears be wiped
away, but the things that cause the tears—death and pain—will be
no more. How can you remember and hold on to that promise?

■ **PRAYER**
Help me, Lord, to hold on to this great hope of a world without tears.
Amen

Romans 5:3–5 (NIV)

Building hope

… but we also glory in our sufferings, because we know that suffering produces perseverance; perseverance, character; and character, hope. And hope does not put us to shame, because God's love has been poured out into our hearts through the Holy Spirit, who has been given to us.

The pressures of life can seem overwhelming. Family problems, financial worries, loss of a close relative or friend—any one of them can drag us down, making life unbearably hard. While one at a time is bad enough, sometimes they come in twos and threes. And if no one else sees the full picture of the pressures we're facing, we can feel desperately alone.

In this Bible passage, Paul puts the pressures we're facing into perspective (the word 'suffering' here refers to pressure). He says that far from leading to despair, pressure can produce hope. Just as diamonds are the product of great pressure, so are godly, hopeful people. The pressure we face is not meaningless—it changes us. Perseverance leads to character and then to hope. And this is not wishful thinking; it's rooted in God; it's an anchor (Hebrews 6:19). As John Stott wrote, 'The reason our hope will never let us down is that God will never let us down.'*

■ PRAYER

Lord, please use the pressures I face to produce perseverance, character and hope in me. May the love you have poured out into me flow out to those I meet today. Amen

* John Stott, *The Message of Romans* (IVP, 1994), p. 142

Isaiah 53:3–4 (NIV)

Jesus knows

He was despised and rejected by mankind, a man of suffering, and familiar with pain. Like one from whom people hide their faces he was despised, and we held him in low esteem. Surely he took up our pain and bore our suffering, yet we considered him punished by God, stricken by him, and afflicted.

At the age of 60 I took a break from work: 'fallow time' I called it, although some friends assumed I'd retired! For the first time I started to understand what it's like not to work. I spent time with friends who were retired, unemployed or on sick leave. Previously I'd tried to *empathise* with people facing those things, imagining what it was like. Now I began to *identify* with their situation—feeling, not just imagining. So when we're in pain it's good to know that Jesus, the servant about whom Isaiah was writing here, understands—he experienced rejection, suffering and pain (v. 3).

But there's more to Jesus' experience than his being able to identify with our difficult experiences. His suffering achieved something concrete for us. He 'took up our pain', 'bore our suffering' (v. 4). In the following verse we see that his suffering brings us forgiveness and healing: 'the punishment that brought us peace was on him, and by his wounds we are healed' (v. 5). He took what we deserved.

■ **PRAYER**

Thank you, Lord Jesus, for bearing the suffering that I deserved. Please help me today to enjoy the freedom your forgiveness brings. Amen

2 Corinthians 4:7–10 (NIV)

Ordinary people

But we have this treasure in jars of clay to show that this all-surpassing power is from God and not from us. We are hard pressed on every side, but not crushed; perplexed, but not in despair; persecuted, but not abandoned; struck down, but not destroyed. We always carry around in our body the death of Jesus, so that the life of Jesus may also be revealed in our body.

Our difficult times may be personal but they're not always private. Other people see how we respond. Recently someone—not a churchgoer—told me about a Christian friend who had faced a series of tragic bereavements. He was amazed how this woman had coped. 'It must be her faith,' he said.

The truth is, most Christians are pretty ordinary people. We're not exceptionally talented or strong; we're just like everyone else—'jars of clay', the most ordinary cooking pots (v. 7). But one thing is different—Jesus, 'the treasure', is in us. So when people see Christians coping under pressure, what they are seeing is 'the life of Jesus' in us (v. 10).

We can be tempted to think that we're too ordinary for God to use. But when others see people like us coping with the pressures of life, they can see that it's because of God's help (or they may say 'your faith').

■ **PRAYER**

Thank you, Lord, for your life in me. As I face today's pressures and trials, please may people around me see you. Amen

Psalm 126:4–6 (NIV)

From tears to joy

Restore our fortunes, Lord, like streams in the Negev. Those who sow with tears will reap with songs of joy. Those who go out weeping, carrying seed to sow, will return with songs of joy, carrying sheaves with them.

When there are no instant solutions to our hard times, keeping going can be difficult. How we long for 'streams in the Negev' (v. 4), which are flash floods. Yet all too often they don't come when we want them. 'How long, Lord?' is a common cry in the Psalms. But the wait doesn't mean that things will never change. This psalm switches to the picture of harvest, which, after a period of sowing, working and waiting, brings with it great joy (v. 6).

This psalm, one of the Songs of Ascents, was written to be sung on a pilgrimage up to Jerusalem. It begins by recalling a time when God acted on behalf of his people (vv. 1–3). They were laughing, singing and full of joy! Remembering what God has done is a good thing to do. Perhaps you have a serious concern or worry for yourself or someone else. Why not take time now to remember God's goodness to you in the past? Then bring today's needs to him, asking that tears will be turned to joy.

■ **PRAYER**

Lord, thank you for the times when you have done great things for me. Please give me the patience and energy to wait for you to act in your good time. Amen

Known and loved

Katherine Hedderly

'I still feel the same as I did when I was eleven,' my 83-year-old mum often tells me. I suppose what she's saying is that she still knows herself to be the same person deep down, although, of course, her life experiences have shaped her, and the physical challenges she lives with mean she's enjoying life in the slow lane now!

Perhaps what she's expressing is a reflection of how God knows us. He knows us through and through, as the psalmist expressed so well in Psalm 139: 'You have searched me and known me' (v. 1, NRSV). God's love recognises the real me, whatever my stage of life. Our identity with God is secure.

In the Old Testament, the people of God struggle with their identity, doubting whether they are really known and loved. They come back to God again and again and are reassured. God remembers them, whatever route they've taken on their journey. We are invited to trust in the knowledge that God is always there for us. In Christ, God's great act of remembering, we can be assured that he will go on knowing, loving and remembering us, 'the real us', because he is 'the same yesterday and today and for ever' (Hebrews 13:8, NRSV). And that's a promise!

Matthew 22:37–39 (NRSV)

A loving disciple

[Jesus] said to him, "'You shall love the Lord your God with all your heart, and with all your soul, and with all your mind." This is the greatest and first commandment. And a second is like it: "You shall love your neighbour as yourself."'

One of the greatest encouragements in our prayer lives is the invitation to start where we are. God meets us there and will journey with us. We just have to take that first step. Perhaps we have experienced a lack of love at times in our lives. But even if our first step with God was many years ago, we each have the chance now to set out afresh in love.

We have to start by loving our neighbour—loving whoever is in our community, loving one another, where we are, right now. And as we do, we begin to know God and discover we are known and loved by him.

And what does love look like? It looks like Jesus, who came to serve, to care for the vulnerable, who was interested in everyone around him, no matter who they were. Love is very human and humble. He is the place of love, where we can begin, or begin again.

■ PRAYER

Lord, show me how to start again with love, love for those you place around me, just where I am. Show me that it is in loving others that I will find you; and in finding you, come to know you. Amen

Psalm 8:3–5 (NRSV)

Crowned with glory

When I look at your heavens, the work of your fingers, the moon and the stars that you have established; what are human beings that you are mindful of them, mortals that you care for them? Yet you have made them a little lower than God, and crowned them with glory and honour.

Maybe you know what it's like to have a garden. Isn't it a joy to be masters of our own small universe, as we sow, plant and tend even the smallest patch into a riot of colour—as well as a tangle of weeds sometimes!

In contrast, we also know those times when we've felt ourselves to be just a tiny part of creation. As a child, I remember looking out at the stars from my bedroom window, and finding it wonderfully and surprisingly comforting, knowing that I was such a small part of so vast a universe. Someone had to be taking care of it all.

God is mindful of us as part of his creation. He gives us freedom to be those who tend and care for it. But he also cares for us when we are feeling very small in it all.

What piece of creation can you cherish and give thanks for today?

■ PRAYER

Lord, show me how to live with the freedom of being part of your beautiful creation. Show me the little things which you take the greatest care of—and so make me mindful of your love. Amen

Genesis 17:4–6 (NRSV)

Called by a new name

'As for me, this is my covenant with you: You shall be the ancestor of a multitude of nations. No longer shall your name be Abram, but your name shall be Abraham… I will make you exceedingly fruitful; and I will make nations of you, and kings shall come from you.'

What is it like to hear your name called by someone you love—a partner, a friend, a son or daughter, a grandchild? I expect you're called by a variety of names. Think about those who you love calling your name.

In the Bible, when God changes a person's name it is to give them a new identity. This is often linked to a new direction to which they are being called, perhaps a new commitment to follow God. With new names, Abraham and Sarah, in their advanced years, step out on a journey of faith together to be a blessing to many. What a challenge!

God has a special name for each one of us who puts our trust in him. Through the prophet Isaiah, God says to his people, 'I have called you by name, you are mine' (Isaiah 43:1b, NRSV). I wonder, as you listen out for God calling your name, what blessings you are being invited to share in?

■ **PRAYER**

Lord, each day you give me opportunities to live up to the name you have given me, whatever my age. Help me to become more and more the person you call me to be. Amen

Matthew 16:13–15 (NRSV)

Growing in confidence

Now when Jesus came into the district of Caesarea Philippi, he asked his disciples, 'Who do people say that the Son of Man is?' And they said, 'Some say John the Baptist, but others Elijah, and still others Jeremiah or one of the prophets.' He said to them, 'But who do you say that I am?'

I wonder, as you get older, if you find yourself able to let go of what others think and trust your own judgement, with the quiet confidence that comes from experience? Jesus had this kind of confidence because he drew on the strength of his Father and knew himself to be his beloved Son.

He wanted his disciples to be confident too for what lay ahead of them. Jesus invited them to trust in what they had learned from their experience of being with him. He wanted to know who *they* thought he was, not everyone else's opinion. If you read on from these verses in Matthew's Gospel, you'll see Peter having the confidence to affirm that Jesus is the Messiah, the Son of God (v. 16).

We too can have this confidence to speak about Jesus, because of the things that we have learned. In what ways do we show that we recognise and know Jesus, in both our words and actions?

■ PRAYER

Lord, give me the confidence to answer your question to me: 'Who do you say that I am?' and rejoice in the answer, in what I do and say. Amen

Ezekiel 47:9 (NRSV)

Lovers of life

Wherever the river goes, every living creature that swarms will live, and there will be very many fish, once these waters reach there. It will become fresh; and everything will live where the river goes.

My mother used to say that once she got to 70 she'd go out to play! She's in her 80s now and, with my father, is still involved in running a Christian Aid group, the Traidcraft stall at their church, and has a monthly lunch group in their home. She hasn't given up all her responsibilities, but she is playful, finding joy, delight and laughter in what she does almost every day—not that life has always been easy for her.

The invitation to each of us, which God offers through the prophet Ezekiel, is to be people who live in the current of life and allow the river of God's love to take us in its flow. God offers us the best of life: the richness of older years, unexpected gifts, relationships, family, experience and time to savour and enjoy them. God wants us to know what it's like to play at all stages of life!

How do you stay in the current? Where are the signs of life around you today?

■ **PRAYER**

Lord God, whatever my circumstances, keep me in the slipstream of life and show me the freshness of your delightful love, so that I may be someone who overflows with joy and love for you and those around me. Amen

John 15:13–15 (NRSV)

A friend of God

No one has greater love than this, to lay down one's life for one's friends. You are my friends if you do what I command you. I do not call you servants any longer, because the servant does not know what the master is doing; but I have called you friends…

We might know people who have laid down their lives in caring for others. I remember Joan, who cared for her husband with Alzheimer's, speaking about the cost of it, but saying: 'We are sure that we know what he needs—company, kind voices, gentle touches, cleanliness, good and tasty food, a comfortable bed. Love.' In providing for his needs day by day, she laid down her life for the one she loved. And God made it possible by bringing all kinds of friends around her to support and sustain her in many helpful and unseen ways.

Jesus relied on his disciples as friends. Do you have friends around you laying down their lives for you in some way? Perhaps you could find ways to tell them how much it is appreciated.

Being a friend of God is a great privilege. We might like to remember the times when God has relied on us to share his friendship with others.

■ PRAYER

Lord, it is in small acts of kindness and gentleness that I recognise the marks of your friendship. Show me how to be someone who makes an imprint of your love on the world today. Amen

Luke 22:19 (NRSV)

God remembers us

Then he took a loaf of bread, and when he had given thanks, he broke it and gave it to them, saying, 'This is my body, which is given for you. Do this in remembrance of me.'

As we grow older we learn the art of letting go. We lay down roles and responsibilities, even those taken up in retirement. We have to face the letting go of loved ones who have accompanied us in our lives. For some it means a letting go of memories through the experience of dementia, or being alongside our dearest ones as that is happening to them. It can be devastating. How do we hold on to our identity and sense of who we are in the face of this? We wonder, 'Who will hold on to the memory of us and those we love when we no longer can?'

At the heart of the Eucharist is God's promise in Jesus never to let go of us. We are always precious and loved in his sight. As a community gathered around the life of Jesus, we are witnesses to his living memory in the world. Through his life we are re-formed as we remember what Jesus did and we act upon it in the present.

In Jesus, God remembers us. We trust that God holds all of our memories, all of who we are. God never lets us go, even in the midst of our letting go.

■ **PRAYER**

Lord Jesus, remember me, when you come into your kingdom. Amen

1 Corinthians 12:24–27 (NRSV)

Together we are one

But God has so arranged the body, giving the greater honour to the inferior member, that there may be no dissension within the body, but the members may have the same care for one another. If one member suffers, all suffer together with it; if one member is honoured, all rejoice together with it. Now you are the body of Christ and individually members of it.

We are who we are because of our relationships with others. *Ubuntu* is the African expression for this. If you've ever played a team sport, you know what it means to say that the team is only as strong as its weakest player. This is the analogy the apostle Paul is using as he encourages the Corinthian church to consider their gifts, which are all of equal worth. In fact, it seems that the weakest members are the most precious.

It can be hard to accept our own weaknesses. But if we think of them as the way God's love can be revealed in our families, our communities, our churches, then we might be less afraid to share them with others. As followers of Jesus, we gather around someone whose ultimate weakness—his death on a cross—was the way to life and hope for the whole world.

■ **PRAYER**

Lord, I often try to cope on my own. As I admit that sometimes I am weak and in need of the support of others, make that a doorway into your kingdom for us all. Amen

1 Corinthians 13:4–8 (NRSV)

Love at our centre

Love is patient; love is kind; love is not envious or boastful or arrogant or rude. It does not insist on its own way; it is not irritable or resentful; it does not rejoice in wrongdoing, but rejoices in the truth. It bears all things, believes all things, hopes all things, endures all things. Love never ends...

At the heart of who we are called to be is the call to be people of love. If we centre ourselves on love, it shapes everything about us. Jean Vanier, the founder of the L'Arche communities, which provide support for those with learning disabilities, says that love doesn't mean doing extraordinary or heroic things; it means knowing how to do ordinary things with tenderness.* This is the kind of Christ-like love the early Christian communities were called to live out, and it was this that set them apart.

A real 'saint' I know told me how she had once turned her elderly father over somewhat roughly in bed, when they were caring for him at home. Although he hadn't noticed, it still troubled her some time later. We might regret some of the ways we have treated others— roughly, not patiently or lovingly. Let's bring these things to God in prayer and commit ourselves to living from a place of love once more.

■ **PRAYER**

Lord, I could never live with love at my centre if you had not first placed it there. Show me how to turn again to living a love-shaped life. Amen

* Jean Vanier, *Community and Growth* (Paulist Press, 1989), p. 298

Psalm 139:1–3 (NRSV)

God knows!

O Lord, you have searched me and known me. You know when I sit down and when I rise up; you discern my thoughts from far away. You search out my path and my lying down, and are acquainted with all my ways.

My grandmother, who lived to 95, was a seamstress. In older age she struggled with rheumatoid arthritis, particularly in her hands, once so nimble and creative. She used to tease me and say, 'Just you wait!' in a loving way, as she shared with me what it felt like to have this physical challenge. It was her way of saying, 'This is real and it's a struggle but I'm living with it, and with humour too!' I wonder if, when she looked at me, then a cheeky ten-year-old, she remembered her own childhood too and the freedom of the 'paths' and 'ways' she had enjoyed then. Psalm 139 tells us that God certainly remembers them.

The words of this psalm are those that we can return to again and again. Let them remind us that God is concerned and aware of even the smallest detail of our lives: our thoughts and feelings, and all that we encounter, day by day, even our sitting down and rising up. There is nothing that is outside his care, whether we are ten or 95!

■ PRAYER

Lord, in holding my life under your loving gaze, I delight in simply being known by you. Show me how to reflect that same love to the world. Amen

Also from
The Bible Reading Fellowship…

This book approaches dementia from a number of angles: biological, psychological, sociological and theological. After an introduction explaining the multifaceted nature of this set of conditions, some possible theological responses are offered to such questions as: what is the nature of human identity? How can someone with severely impaired cognition have a full spiritual life?

Thinking of You
A resource for the spiritual care of people with dementia
Joanna Collicutt
978 0 85746 491 0 £9.99
brfonline.org.uk

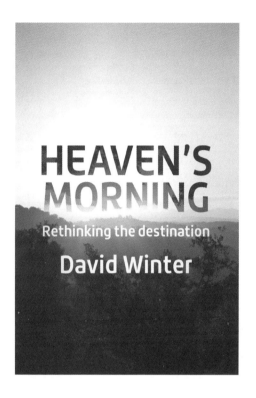

The Bible—especially the New Testament—has plenty to say about resurrection and heaven, but many Christians struggle to make sense of what it actually means in practice. David Winter's accessible book explores the biblical teaching on what happens after death and considers what difference this can make to our lives here and now. He also shows how we can present what we believe about eternity as a source of hope to our sceptical, anxious world.

Heaven's Morning
Rethinking the destination
David Winter
978 0 85746 476 7   £7.99
brfonline.org.uk

To order

Online: **brfonline.org.uk**
Telephone: +44 (0)1865 319700
Mon–Fri 9.15–17.30
Post: complete this form and send to the address below

Delivery times within the UK are normally 15 working days. Prices are correct at the time of going to press but may change without prior notice.

Title	Issue*	Price	Qty	Total
Postcards from Heaven		£7.99		
Thinking of You		£9.99		
Heaven's Morning		£7.99		
Bible Reflections for Older People (single copy)	May/Sep* 17	£4.99		
Bible Reflections for Older People (10–24 copies)	May/Sep* 17	£4.75		
Bible Reflections for Older People (25–49 copies)	May/Sep* 17	£4.50		
Bible Reflections for Older People (50 or more copies)	May/Sep* 17	£3.99		

delete as appropriate

POSTAGE AND PACKING CHARGES			
Order value	UK	Europe	Rest of world
Under £7.00	£1.25	£3.00	£5.50
£7.00–29.99	£2.25	£5.50	£10.00
£30.00 and over	FREE	Prices on request	

Total value of books	
Postage and packing	
Total for this order	

Please complete in BLOCK CAPITALS

Title .... First name/initials .... Surname..

Address ....

.... Postcode ....

Acc. No. .... Telephone ....

Email ....

Method of payment

❑ Cheque (made payable to BRF) ❑ MasterCard / Visa

Card no. ☐☐☐☐ ☐☐☐☐ ☐☐☐☐ ☐☐☐☐

Valid from M M Y Y Expires M M Y Y Security code* ☐☐☐
Last 3 digits on the reverse of the card

Signature* .... Date .... / .... / ....
*ESSENTIAL IN ORDER TO PROCESS YOUR ORDER

Please return this form to:

BRF, 15 The Chambers, Vineyard, Abingdon OX14 3FE | enquiries@brf.org.uk
To read our terms and conditions, please visit **brfonline.org.uk/terms**.

The Bible Reading Fellowship (BRF) is a Registered Charity (233280)

BIBLE REFLECTIONS FOR OLDER PEOPLE GROUP SUBSCRIPTION FORM

> All our Bible reading notes can be ordered online
> by visiting **biblereadingnotes.org.uk/subscriptions**

The group subscription rate for *Bible Reflections for Older People* will be £14.97 per person until August 2018.

☐ I would like to take out a group subscription for .... (*quantity*) copies.

☐ Please start my order with the September 2017 / January 2018 / May 2018* issue. I would like to pay annually/receive an invoice with each edition of the notes.* (*delete as appropriate*)

Please do not send any money with your order. Send your order to BRF and we will send you an invoice. The group subscription year is from 1 May to 30 April. If you start subscribing in the middle of a subscription year we will invoice you for the remaining number of issues left in that year.

Name and address of the person organising the group subscription:

Title .... First name/initials .... Surname ....

Address ....

.... Postcode ....

Telephone .... Email ....

Church ....

Name of minister ....

Name and address of the person paying the invoice if the invoice needs to be sent directly to them:

Title .... First name/initials .... Surname ....

Address ....

.... Postcode ....

Telephone .... Email ....

Please return this form to:
BRF, 15 The Chambers, Vineyard, Abingdon OX14 3FE | enquiries@brf.org.uk
To read our terms and conditions, please visit **brfonline.org.uk/terms**.

BROP0217

The Bible Reading Fellowship is a Registered Charity (233280)

BIBLE REFLECTIONS FOR OLDER PEOPLE INDIVIDUAL/GIFT SUBSCRIPTION FORM

> To order online, please visit **biblereadingnotes.org.uk/subscriptions**

☐ I would like to take out a subscription (*complete your name and address details only once*)
☐ I would like to give a gift subscription (*please provide both names and addresses*)

Title .... First name/initials .... Surname.....................................

Address ....

.... Postcode ....

Telephone .... Email ....

Gift subscription name ....

Gift subscription address ....

.... Postcode ....

Gift message (*20 words max. or include your own gift card*):

....

....

Please send *Bible Reflections for Older People* beginning with the September 2017 / January 2018 / May 2018* issue (*delete as appropriate*):

(*please tick box*)	UK	Europe	Rest of world
Bible Reflections for Older People	☐ £18.75	☐ £26.70	☐ £30.75

Total enclosed £ .... (*cheques should be made payable to 'BRF'*)

Please charge my MasterCard / Visa ☐ Debit card ☐ with £ ....

Card no. ☐☐☐☐ ☐☐☐☐ ☐☐☐☐ ☐☐☐☐

Valid from M M Y Y   Expires M M Y Y   Security code* ☐☐☐
Last 3 digits on the reverse of the card

Signature* .... Date ...... / ...... / ......
*ESSENTIAL IN ORDER TO PROCESS YOUR ORDER

Please return this form to:
BRF, 15 The Chambers, Vineyard, Abingdon OX14 3FE | enquiries@brf.org.uk
To read our terms and conditions, please visit **brfonline.org.uk/terms**.